For a Girl Becoming

VOLUME 66

SUN TRACKS

An American Indian Literary Series

Series Editor

Ofelia Zepeda

Editorial Committee

Larry Evers

Joy Harjo

Geary Hobson

N. Scott Momaday

Irvin Morris

Simon J. Ortiz

Kate Shanley

Leslie Marmon Silko

Luci Tapahonso

For a Girl Becoming

Written by
JOY HARJO

Illustrations by
Mercedes McDonald

THE UNIVERSITY OF ARIZONA PRESS

Tucson

The University of Arizona Press
Text © 2009 by Joy Harjo
Illustrations © 2009 by Mercedes McDonald
All rights reserved

www.uapress.arizona.edu

Library of Congress Cataloging-in-Publication Data
appear on the last printed page of this book.

Publication of this book is made possible in part by the proceeds of a
permanent endowment created with the assistance of a Challenge Grant
from the National Endowment for the Humanities, a federal agency.

Printed in Korea through Four Colour Print Group, Louisville, Kentucky

Printing Plant Location: Printed by We SP Corp., Seoul, Korea)
Production Date: 10-22-2019
Job / Batch #: 85174

For a Girl Becoming

That day your spirit came to us,

rains came in from the Pacific to bless.

Clouds peered over the mountains

in response to the singing of medicine plants,

who danced back and forth in shawls of mist.

Your mother labored there, so young in earthly years.

Your father and all of us who loved you gathered

where pollen blew throughout that desert house to bless.

Horses were running the land, hundreds of them.

They accompanied you here, to bless.

Girl, I wonder what you thought as you paused there in your spirit house,

before you entered into the breathing world to be with us?

Were you longing for us, too?

Our relatives in that beloved place dressed you in black hair,

brown eyes, and skin the color of earth.

They turned you in this direction.

We want you to know that we urgently gathered to welcome you here.

We came bearing gifts to celebrate:

From your mother's house we brought poetry, music, medicine
makers, stubbornness, beauty, tribal leaders, and a yard filled
with junked cars and the gift of knowing how to make them run.
We carried tobacco and cedar, new clothes and joy for you.

And from your father's house came
educators, thinkers, dreamers,
weavers, and mathematical genius.

They carried a cradleboard,
hope, white shell,
and turquoise for you.
We brought blankets to
wrap you in and soft,
beaded moccasins
of deerskin.

Did you hear us as you traveled from your rainbow house?

We called you with thunder, with singing.

Did you see us as we gathered in the town beneath the mountains?

We were dressed in concern and happiness.

We were overwhelmed with awe as you moved through the weft of
your mother.

Even before you took your first breath, your eyes blinked wide open.

Now, breathe.

And when you breathe, remember the source of the gift of all breathing.

When you walk, remember the source of the gift of all walking.

And when you run, remember the source of the gift of all running.

And when you laugh, remember the source of the gift of all laughter.

And when you cry, remember the source of the gift of all tears.

And when you dream, remember the source of the gift of all dreaming.

And when your heart is broken, remember the source of the gift of all breaking.

And when your heart is put back together, remember the source of all putting back together.

Don't forget how you started your journey from that rainbow house, how you traveled and will travel through the mountains and valleys of human tests.

There are treacherous places along the way, but you can come to us.

There are lakes of tears shimmering sadly there, but you can come to us.

And valleys without horses or kindness, but you can come to us.

And angry, jealous gods and wayward humans who will hurt you, but
you can come to us.

You will fall and you will get back up again, because you are one of us.

And as you travel with us, remember all this:

Give a drink of water to all who ask, whether they be plant, creature, human, or helpful spirit.

May you always have clean, fresh water.

Feed your neighbors. Give kind words and assistance

to all you meet along the way—

We are all related in this place—

May you be surrounded with the helpfulness of family and good friends.

Grieve with the grieving, share joy with the joyful.

May you build a strong path with beautiful and truthful language.

Clean your room.

May you always have a home: a refuge from storm, a gathering-place
    for safety, for comfort.

Bury what needs to be buried.

Laugh easily at yourself; may you always travel lightly and well.

Praise and give thanks for each small and large thing.

May you grow in knowledge, in compassion, and beauty.

Always within you is that day your spirit came to us.

When rains came in from the Pacific to bless.

Clouds peered over the mountains

in response to the singing of medicine plants,

who danced back and forth in shawls of mist.

Your mother labored there, so young in earthly years.

And we who love you gather here.

Pollen blows throughout this desert house to bless.

And horses run the land, hundreds of them, for you.

And you are here to bless.

About the Author

PAUL ABDOO

JOY HARJO was born in Tulsa, Oklahoma, and is a member of the Mvskoke (Creek) Nation. Her seven books of poetry include *She Had Some Horses*, *The Woman Who Fell From the Sky*, and *How We Became Human, New and Selected Poems*. Her poetry has garnered many awards including a Lila Wallace–Reader's Digest Award, the New Mexico Governor's Award for Excellence in the Arts, the Lifetime Achievement Award from the Native Writers Circle of the Americas, and the William Carlos Williams Award from the Poetry Society of America. She has released three award-winning CDs of original music and performances: *Letter from the End of the Twentieth Century*, *Native Joy for Real*, and *She Had Some Horses*. Her most recent CD of music, *Winding Through the Milky Way*, won the Outstanding Musical Achievement award from the First Americans in the Arts. She has received the Eagle Spirit Achievement Award for overall contributions in the arts from the American Indian Film Festival. She performs internationally solo and with her band, Joy Harjo and the Arrow Dynamics Band (for which she sings and plays saxophone and flutes). Her first reading of her one-woman show, *Wings of Night Sky, Wings of Morning Light*, was featured at the Public Theater in New York. The world premiere of the play was produced by Native Voices at the Autry in Los Angeles Spring 2009. She co-wrote the signature film of the National Museum of the American Indian, *A Thousand Roads*. She is a founding board member of the Native Arts and Cultures Foundation. Harjo writes a column, "Comings and Goings," for her tribal newspaper, the *Muscogee Nation News*. She lives in Albuquerque, New Mexico, and Honolulu, Hawai'i, where she is a member of the Hui Nalu Canoe Club.

About the Illustrator

MERCEDES McDONALD is a successful and well-known freelance illustrator. Her artistic style is characterized by vivid color imagery in pastels that depict her childhood memories of the West and often feature animals. She further developed and refined her natural artistic talent at the Atlanta College of Art, the California College of Arts and Crafts, and the San Francisco Art Institute, where she earned an M.F.A. in painting. She has worked with Chronicle Books, Harcourt Brace, and other publishers for whom she has illustrated numerous books, such as *How Snake Got His Hiss: An Original Tale* (Orchard Books, 1996) and *Fairy Trails: A Story Told in English and Spanish* (Bloomsbury Publishing PLC, 2005). In 1990, McDonald received the Maxwell Award for her drawings in *Cooking with Dogs* (Dig Writer's Association of America, 1998) and has been featured in *Communication Arts Magazine*. Her latest book *Hola Noche/Hello Night* received the International Book Award for Best Bilingual Picture Book of 2008. McDonald taught illustration at the California College of Arts and Crafts in San Francisco for six years. She is now an adjunct faculty at the College of the Canyons in Valencia, California, and at California State University, Fullerton.

Library of Congress Cataloging-in-Publication Data

Harjo, Joy.
For a girl becoming / written by Joy Harjo ;
illustrated by Mercedes McDonald.
p. cm.
ISBN 978-0-8165-2797-7 (cloth : alk. paper)
1. Indian girls—Juvenile poetry. 2. Indians
of North America—Juvenile poetry. 3. Children's
poetry, American. I. McDonald, Mercedes, ill.
II. Title.
PS3558.A62423F67 2009
811'.54—dc22   2009009847

Design and composition: Barbara Haines
Text: Warnock Pro   Display: Ovidius